"There will be

But in the days when the seventh angel is about to sound his trumpet,
the mystery of God will be accomplished, just as He announced to his servants the prophets."

Then the voice that I heard from heaven spoke to me once more:

"Go, take the scroll that lies in the hand of the angel standing on the sea and on the land"
Rev.10:7&8

A Message from the book of Revelation

Written by Elisabeth Heeley

In obedience to the Sovereign Lord

Dedicated to:

All who believes

In God the Father as Creator,

His Son, Jesus Christ

And the Holy Spirit.

May the reader be blessed as you read

the "scroll"

The Introduction

Many years ago, an angel told Daniel to seal the revelation God gave him concerning the end times, just before the return of Jesus Christ.

Then we read that Jesus "unsealed" - the scroll for us to read what will happen at the end of the age according to the prophetic book, Revelation, which was written by the apostle John.

John, the beloved disciple of Jesus, was persecuted by Roman soldiers and was sent to the Isle of Patmos. During a time of separation from other Believers, aged and perhaps in pain, he had a revelation of Jesus. He also had visions of the heavenly battles and what will happen on earth, before the second coming of Jesus.

These visions or "pictures" might look strange to us in the modern era, but these visions have spiritual meaning and the angel of the Lord explained the visions and today the Holy Spirit gives us understanding about the prophetic book.

> I hope to shine more light on the book of Revelation and reveal the message to readers who might be the last generation, the generation that will witness the second coming of Jesus!

This Book is written

In three parts:

Part 1-The Last Message to the Church

Part 2- The Anti-Christ and judgments

Part 3 – Jesus Christ, the coming King!

Best to have a Bible open right next to you, while reading this booklet. You also might need a notebook too, while discovering the message in this "scroll".

Part one

The Last Message To The Church

2020~

Chapter One

Apostle John wrote to the servants of God about the revelation of Jesus Christ and what soon must take place. "Soon", is a relative word which means soon from God's point of view and soon for a prophet who experienced the visions and message from God as a "now" word! The word "soon" also has a message for each generation from the book of Revelation. We only live once and each generation has to overcome their obstacles and be prepared to meet the King of kings! So when people reading this book of Revelation, Father God wants that generation to get ready for the return of his Son, Jesus Christ. It is for-told that many more people will research this book before the return of Jesus Christ. As for now, more and more books are written about the book of Revelation. For the last 50 years many people started to read the book of Revelations, searching through the scriptures to understand this prophetic book. My grandchild of nine, asked my daughter to read the Book of Revelation to her. Many years ago, believers did not even attempt to read this book. It was then too complicated, but now, the Holy Spirit opening our eyes and minds to understand; to see Jesus as the risen Lord and victorious King!

The angel instructed John to write down what he saw and then he must send it to seven churches (assemblies or gatherings) What did he see? At first, he saw seven golden lampstands and amongst it, a man standing, dressed in a long robe with a golden sash around his chest. In those days royalty wore long robes. Working class and servants wore short tunics. Usually athletes, who took part in a race or some competition, received a golden sash when they won the race or competition. Jesus won the victory over Satan, sin and death!

Let us continue looking at the vision John saw of Jesus, as the victorious, risen Lord and King. The "son of Man" meaning a human being. His head were like white wool and his eyes were like blazing fire-torches. According to King Solomon's proverbs, white hair symbolize wisdom that most elderly have after years of experienced life. The meaning of eyes like fire: his eyes that penetrates through the souls of mankind, knowing our thoughts and motives of our hearts.

His feet were like bronze glowing in a furnace. Bronze is the colour of sin. This time, Jesus is not dress as a servant, but wherever he goes, He will judge sin. He is like a purifying fire! He will weighing, judge and burn up sin, just as fire consumes everything that cannot withstand the test of fire.

John heard his voice. Like rushing waters (a big waterfall). It reminds me of the words Jesus spoke at the feast of Tabernacles, recorded in the gospel of John: **"If anybody is thirsty, come and drink from the water I give. Out of your belly, living waters will well up…"** Jesus also said to the Samaritan woman at the well: **"The water I give, you shall never thirst again …"** The words Jesus speaks, are refreshing, comforting and brings forth healing and everlasting life.

Are you getting a picture of Jesus, who is now, at the right Hand of God the Father?
John also saw that Jesus held the seven stars in his right hand: meaning that God's messengers, are like angels in his hands. He upholds his words in their mouths. The prophets and those who prophesy and preach a message to the Churches are Gifts in the hands of God. Just as Jesus is the Word of God, so are those who speaks on behalf of God, bringing His Word to the churches!

And then, I was disturbed by what Apostle John saw next: A double edged sword coming forth from his mouth! John fell down like one who is dead! I asked the Lord, how can this be, your voice like many waters and also like a double edged sword?! And then Jesus said to me: If you want to shower, you go and stand under the water. **My voice is like many waters to those who receive my word, to those who want it, those who**

come to be saved, for those who come to be healed and to those who need refreshing, I will be like a waterfall of living waters to them. But to the world, my words are like a sword: "For the word of God is living and active. Sharper than a two edged sword, it penetrates even to dividing soul and spirit, joints and marrow; it judges the thoughts and attitudes of the heart." Hebrew 4:12.

Jesus said to John: "**Do not be afraid. I am the First and the Last. I am the living One. I was dead, but I am alive forever and ever. Write down what you see and send it to the seven churches in Asia**" We all agree that John had a vision of Jesus as the risen Lord, the victorious one over Satan, sin and death! What was Jesus saying to the seven churches? In the next two chapters we shall read what Jesus said about seven churches in Asia, which still hold a message and promise for us today.

In the Gospels we read that Jesus was born as a human being, the son of man.
He came to serve the Israelites, to show the believers God the Father; to pay for our sins and to make a way back for us to have fellowship with God again like Adam and Eve had from the beginning. Jesus entered Jerusalem on a donkey, which symbolized His humility and that he came to serve. But when

Jesus will come again, He shall come as a righteous King to judge those who continue sinning; who stand far off; those who rebelled against Him and ignored the message of God's servants.

Jesus is coming back to redeem those who belong to Him. He will reign for a thousand years on earth. Every believer who overcome the sin and temptations of this world and did the will of God, shall reign with Him. Will you reign with Him or will you be judge?

Chapter Two

What was Jesus saying to the seven churches and why seven and not more or less?

The number seven in the Hebrew numerical means completion. After God created the world, He rested on the seventh day. We read that the Holy Spirit is a seven-fold Spirit around God's throne. God's vengeance of the nations, during the tribulation will be seven years. There are many things in the book of Revelation which are seven times. It also means wholeness. It is God's number!

Many authors, like Hal Lindsay, Mark Hitchcock and Billy Graham agreed that the seven churches represent the general church of Jesus Christ over the years, started at the time when the Holy Spirit was poured out upon the Believers in Jesus Christ. Please read chapter 2 of the book of Acts, written 2000 years ago.

What can we learn from these letters to the seven churches? What is the NOW message for us?!

I remember apostle Paul wrote that we are an open letter for the world to read. What will the people read when they look at you? Let us make these letters personal: What would Jesus say about your relationship with Him and how do you serve God?

In the book of Samuel, we read that Eli failed to discipline his two sons, and God said He will rise up for himself a faithful priest that will do according to what is in His heart and mind. 1Sam.2:35

What did Jesus say about the Church in Ephesus?
He revealed Himself here as the one who holds the seven stars in His right hand (stars- the messengers or angels of the churches) and who walks between the seven churches. (the golden lampstands). When Jesus said: He holds the seven stars in His right hand – it means that the messengers, who delivered His word to the churches, represent Him, Jesus the living Word of God, carries authority.

He says, "I know you do not tolerate wicked people. You have tested those who claim to be apostles, but are not."
When is a person an apostle and when not? There are many people who titled themselves as an "Apostle" but their ministry does not show it. I asked the Lord this question and He answered: An Apostle has seen Jesus. (Whether in real life or in a vision.) They can do miracles; See Acts 5:12 and chapter 9:40 –

Peter brought Dorcas back to life!

They have authority over life and death (when Peter told Ananias that he would die because he lied.) God gives apostles a mandate, a plan what to do like a Moses. He had to build a Tabernacle. Paul had to go and teach a doctrine of faith, that we are saved by grace; that gentiles are also part of God's chosen people.

An apostle has many gives: can teach, preach and pastor and delegate work to others –overseen a group of people. It does not mean he has to do everything, but he can and can appoint the right person for the job.

Jesus said he holds against the church of Ephesus that they had forsaken their first love. He required repentance and do again what they did first. See verse 5. If they do not repent, He shall remove the church! (their light will go out) **But if they repent from their lack of love and yield to the Holy Spirit, they shall eat from the Tree of Life!**

The message to the church in Smyrna:

Jesus introduced himself as the First and the Last, who died and is now alive. The words of Him who is the First and the Last- so much authority, He makes me stand to my feet! He is sovereign and has my full attention!

"I know your afflictions" Jesus knew that they were slandered, betrayed by their own native people. He encouraged them not to give up and not be afraid of suffering. Jesus also warned his disciples of the hard time that will come upon the whole earth. See Matthew 24:21. The devil who is behind all the persecution, will cause many followers of Jesus to be imprisoned and suffer and some may die. Jesus said to be faithful to the point of death. Do not give up or disown Jesus under pressure. Those who endure and hold on to their faith shall reign with Christ during the millennium. To those who win, the Overcomers, shall receive a crown of Life, which means, they shall bring honor and glory to God through their life-style on earth.

The message to the church in Perganum:

The angel introduced Jesus to the church: these are the words of Him who has **the sharp, double edged sword.**

The church was situated in a cultured city full of idol worship. There was a temple built in honor of Ceaser Octavius and an altar to the honor of their god, Zeus. Many Christians suffered and died, like Antipas, a faithful witness of Jesus Christ.

Jesus held it against them that there were people who were influenced by the teaching of Balaam that led them to eat food that was offered to gods and then to sexual immorality. There were those who also held on to the teachings of Nicholas, the deacon who was influenced by Greek beliefs.

So how would we know what to avoid and what are the right teachings we should learn? Simply, since we are followers of Jesus Christ we should teach what He taught His disciples. **Start reading and meditate on the four Gospels: Mathew, Mark, Luke and John.** Learn the words Jesus said and do what he did. Being a follower of Jesus, I have done some similar things Jesus did, preached about the Kingdom of God, taught and making disciples of Jesus; multiplied food, healed the sick and done some miracles. I aspire to become more like Him. Jesus is the first born son of God and we are His brothers and sisters if we continue being led by the Spirit and doing the same works He did.

To the Church of Thyatira: To the angel of the church – these are the words of **the Son of God, whose eyes are like blazing fire and feet are like burning bronze!**

This church was a very busy church doing many good works, serving God and people. But they tolerated and allowing a woman misleading God's servants into sexual immorality through her teachings! She had a spirit of idolatry and impurity.

She called herself a prophetess. She allured believers away from the living God by gratifying their fleshy desires. So God gave her time to repent, but she didn't so He caused her to suffer and also those who submitted to her teachings, they suffered too. Therefore a leader of a church needs to make sure their teachers and preachers live a holy life and investigate what are their fruit in their lives? Look at their family, children and friends. The fruit of a godly servant of God are of peace and health to those around them; a people who are blessed, because they are friends with a servant of God.

When I was chosen to be a principle of a Christian private school, none of my people or teachers was ill during the swine epidemic in South-Africa. All the schools were closed for so many pupils were sick. But my students and teachers were well and our school continued, because God gave me wisdom how to protect them. And they obeyed and stayed healthy.

Jesus said: **"To him who overcomes and do my will, I will give authority over the nations"**. Rev.2:26. The Body of Christ with the strong arm of the Lord: "He will rule them with an iron scepter."   God always works through his servants, His chosen ones.

The above verses remind me of **Psalm 2**, where God challenged

King David: **"Ask of me, and I will give you the nations!"**

I usually pray faithfully for my family, for the church leaders and government, but now also for all nations. To faithfully pray for your government and church leaders, one has to schedule time during the week to do so. Apostle Paul exhorted Timothy to pray for everyone, but especially for leaders in authority, so that we may live peaceful lives in all godliness and holiness.

Chapter Three

To the angel of the church in Sardis: These are the words of Him who holds the seven Spirits of God and the seven stars.

Jesus said that they have the reputation of being alive, but are dead. Wake up!

There are many churches, Evangelical and charismatic gatherings who sing out loud praises to God, clap their hands and who are involve with community services, but that does not proof that they are alive in Christ, doing the work God has preplanned for them to do. According to Ephesians chapter 2:10 our good works must come from our communication with God and out of a relationship with Him, doing the works He has preplanned for us. Thus hearing Gods word and keeping in step with the Holy Spirit. We must do the will of God. If people suggest you get involve with something, asking yourself is it in line with my calling, is it in line with the vision of our church and is it God's will for me to do?

In the Good News book of John chapter fifteen, it is written that "if you remain in Me and my words remain in you – you shall bear much fruit." We can do works and nice deeds to be promoted in the community and to impress the town council, but it could not be the good deeds God wants us to do. Usually members with a prophetic gift, those seers will know which way their church should go. People will recognize your gift, the good works you should do.

Jesus acknowledged those people in Sardis who kept their clothes clean, meaning they did not get involve with the wrong works. They serve according to God's plan and will. They serve God and fulfill their calling in a holy manner and not according to the world standard.

He who overcomes will be dressed in white and their names will be acknowledged before my Father and his angels.

To the angel of the church in Philadelphia:
The name - Philadelphia means "Brotherly love"

These are the words of **Him who is holy and true** and who holds the key of David. I believe the key of David means, the authority king David had to reign over his enemies. The same covenant God made with King David, Jesus also made with this church. He will make those who lied and betrayed them, to bow before them and acknowledge that Jesus loved them.

What Jesus opens no one can shut and what he shuts, no-one can opens. I believe the open door means Believers who go out to conquer areas and witness to people about Jesus. They were a church who evangelized. According to Hal Lindsey, it was a church on God's time-line: it was a time when many missionaries were sent out. There were a great awakening and the need for Christian universities to be established. Revival swept across English speaking countries.

Jesus promised to them that He shall keep them from the hour of trial that is coming upon the whole world. It could mean that God will save them, like He did in the time of Noah or like when He sent an angel to rescued Lot and his family before the city was destroyed. This prophecy has not taken place yet. Thus it must be a church group that still exist, who pleases the Lord. Jesus encouraged them to hold on to what they have and keep their crown of authority and identity. Those who overcome their enemies will have an eternal place in the spiritual temple in the New Jerusalem. They shall also have a new name.

I find it very interesting that a similar prophecy was given to the prophet Isaiah. He recorded it in chapter 56: 4&5. For those who hold fast to the Lord's covenant, will be given a memorial and an everlasting name! This is the wonder of this book of

Revelation, that it has similarities with other books, like Daniel and Ezekiel and other prophetic books. He who has an ear, must hear what the Spirit is saying to the Churches!

To the angel of the church in Laodicea: These are the words of the **Amen, the Faithful and True Witness, the Ruler of God's creation.**

I remember in Genesis, Moses wrote: God commanded Adam and Eve to rule over the animals in the sea, in the sky and on the land and to take care of the earth. We are created in God's image. So here in Revelation, the Son of Man is called the Ruler of God's creation. It is actually the Word of God that should rule the earth; the word of God in our mouths! Not the Prince of the air who influences our minds and souls.

We should be a people with zeal, like flames of fire, (Ps.104:4) like Jesus with a two edged sword in his mouth. (Rev.1:16 and 19:15).

Jesus said He would rather have a people who are cold hearted than lukewarm. There is nothing worse than to drink lukewarm water, or tea that cooled down!

Jesus holds against this church that they trusted in mere humans for their health and put their security in money, their jobs and education! Jesus said: "You do not realize that you are pitiful, poor, blind and naked! Jesus invites them to come and buy true riches from Him: Gold, that represent godly wisdom; white fine clothes, are the good deeds that was pre-planned for you to do when the world were created (Eph.1:4) the salve on the eyes, are the anointing of the Holy Spirit! True riches are wisdom, the fear of God that will gain a long life, wealth, honor and the respect from people in your sphere of influence.

Jesus said to **"Those I love, I rebuke and discipline. Therefore Repent!"** Afterwards, He comforts and always reaches out to us... these famous words: **"Here I am! I stand at the door and knock. If anyone hears my voice and opens the door, I will come in** and **eat with him and he with me. To him who overcomes, I will give the right to sit with me on my throne, just as I overcame and sit down with my Father on his throne!"**

Such a privilege to have the Savior residence in your home! Jesus wants to be a part of your life. And then the sure promise that when we have victory over sin, Satan and situations, we shall reign with Christ, seated on heavenly thrones next to Him! Hallelujah!

Chapter Four

After Jesus called the churches to repentance, John saw a door standing open in heaven. John heard the same voice described in chapter one, sounded like a trumpet, said: "Come up here, and I will show you what must take place after this!" This open door says it all: **You are welcome, come in to the throne room of Almighty God!** John was getting a viewing of what was taken place in the center of heaven! And now, we too may know and see how it looks around God's throne.

At once John was in the Spirit and saw a throne in heaven with Someone sitting on it. Please take note that Spirit was written in a capital letter, meaning Holy Spirit. John was in the Spirit in heavenly places. God is Spirit, therefore to have fellowship with Him, we need to become one in the Holy Spirit with God.

The beloved apostle described the One who sat on the throne encircled with a rainbow. There were twenty four elders in white garments surrounding the throne. White garments that represent their purity. They did not soil their clothes with the sins of the world. Remember we read about that in Revelation chapter three. They had golden crowns on their heads. It is their crown of life and of righteousness we read also about it chapters two and three. From the throne came flashes of lighting and rumblings of thunder. In front of the throne were seven lamps blazing. They were the seven spirits of God, represent the Holy Spirit! Take note that it is the number seven again. The Holy Spirit functions in different spheres: He is active and alive with in people, sound, light, water and gasses, under the earth and above the earth. Because the Spirit of God functions in many forms and works in different places, one wants to speak of the Holy Spirit in the female form, although theologically we speak of God's Spirit as a He, we must remember God is a Spirit and has no gender, He is not bound to male nor a female form.

In front of the throne was like a sea of glass – transparent like crystal. Actually, I saw that in a spiritual dream when Jesus shared with me concerning worship. Jesus took my hand and led me across the sea of glass to a thick, massive heavy wine- red curtain. I had to take my shoes off. Jesus gave me rainbow colored soft slippers to wear. The curtain was pulled open and Jesus revealed to me how the church worship looked like at that time. I was in shocked as Jesus shown me an image behind the curtain! (And now, I'm weeping while revealing this revelation) I saw a calf-dog- animal like image, made of clay, bronze, copper and iron. It was horrible! I was horrified and also very surprised that our worship, which I thought was good, in fact smart, was looking like that in the heavenly places with Jesus! Suddenly I realized our musicians need to get their music from the throne room from God. Let us practice at home to enter God's presence, so to receive what He has in store for us here and now.

In the center, near the throne, were four living creatures: a lion, an ox, a human being and an eagle; they were covered with many eyes all over them. This means it was spiritual beings that were all knowing and all seeing, nothing was hidden from them. In the book of the prophet, Ezekiel chapter one, we also read about these same four creatures! I was schooled that these creatures represent four different styles of ministries: The eagle, the visionary who sees the bigger picture and received his plans by hearing from God. Then the ox, represent the domestic animals, but spiritually those who serve by praying and preparing practically what needs to be done. The human being is the Son of man on earth, connecting with and serving other people and the lion, as head of the wild animals, could represent the prophetic and evangelist voice, proclaiming what

God is saying. There were no fish, because their habitat is water. These creatures were worshiping Him, day and night:

> "Holy, holy, holy
> is the Lord God Almighty,
> who was, and is, and is to come"

All these creatures were honoring and glorifying Him who sits on the throne! Also the twenty four elders, who were royal priest, would lay down their crowns and worship Him, saying:

> "You are worthy, our Lord and God,
> to receive glory and honor and power,
> for you created all things,
> and by your will they were created
> and have their being."

Worship is the main action in heaven. God is so Awesome, one cannot other than worship Him. The door is standing open for you too. What would you do and what would you sing?

Chapter Five

We are looking at the Book of Revelation, chapter five. Apostle John wrote that he saw a scroll in the right hand of Him who sits upon the throne in heaven. The scroll was sealed with seven seals. In the book of Daniel, that was written about four thousand years ago, we read about the angel who appeared to Daniel and told him to seal the scroll. It was about the end times, what will happen just before the return of Jesus Christ. Then later, two thousand years ago, Jesus told his disciples in Matthew 24, briefly what will happen. The angel in the book of Revelation also revealed to John what will happen.

A mighty angel asked: **"Who is worthy to open the seals?"** The time has come for us to know what was written in the scroll, so we can prepare and get ready for the return of Jesus Christ. John desperately wanted to know what was written in the scroll and there seems to be no one worthy to open the seven sealed scroll! John wept...then an elder said:" Do not weep; the Lion of Judah has triumphed and will open the scroll". Please note the metaphor between humans and animals. John saw a Lamb as if it had be slain, standing in the center, in front of the throne. He had seven horns and seven eyes, which are the seven spirits of God who were sent out into all the earth.

The Lamb came and took the scroll from Him who sits upon the throne. With this, the four creatures and the twenty-four elders fell down before the Lamb who is worthy to open the scroll and the seven seals.

Each one had a harp and golden bowls full of incense, which are the prayers of the saints. Take note that our prayers are like incense before the Lord God and kept in golden bowls! The harps are the string instruments they play as they worship the One who sits upon the throne. They sang a new song: **"You are worthy to take the scroll and open its seals, because you were slain, and with your Blood you purchased men for God from every tribe and language and people and nation. You have made them to be a kingdom and priests to serve our God and they will reign on the earth."**

The new song is the NOW song. It is the song the Holy Spirit gives after you have received the word from God and the revelation from the Holy Spirit. Many years ago, the Lord encouraged me to sing the new song. At first I did not understand what it was, but when I shared a prophetic message at a church in Kilmartin, Scotland, in 2009, a man stood up with a his guitar and sang a new song, the song the Holy Spirit gave him while I was speaking, and God said: "That is the New song!"

Many angels, thousands upon thousands sang**: "Worthy is the Lamb who was slain to receive power and wealth and wisdom and strength and honour and glory and praise**!"

After that, all the creatures in heaven and on earth and in the sea, sang: "To Him who sits on the throne and unto the Lamb be praise and honour and glory and power, forever and ever!" The four living creatures and the twenty four elders fell down and worshipped Him!

The Lamb opened the first of the seven seals. One of the four creatures said, "Come!" And I looked and before me was a white horse! The rider was given a crown and held a bow. He rode out as a conqueror bent on a conquest ...

Some say that it is the Anti-Christ. But God and His angels will not send out the Anti-Christ! I say it represents God's servant with a crown (as we have read in the previous chapters) and bow (with arrows) who wants to advance the kingdom of God. First God's word goes out: the evangelists, prophets and Christians with an apostolic anointing. Many will have the chance to receive God's word and repent, like we see today are taking place in South of Ethiopia and in Syria. But when they harden their hearts, the following "Horses" go out. Please read Revelation chapter six.

As the Lamb opens the next seals, we will know what is going to happen before Jesus, coming as the Judge on a white horse. You can read about that in Revelation chapter 19 and we shall later discuss this in my book. We read about King Jehu who rode out on a horse on a quest to put an end to Queen Jezebel, the false prophetess. We also read in Psalms how King David rode out with his bow in hand against God's enemies! No where do we read that the Anti-christ rides a white horse. There is no other Biblical proof of that. So, we can believe that he who rides a white horse is a Messenger and a follower of Jesus who does ride a white horse.

I believe now is the time for all to make friends with God. Do accept the offer of Life Jesus made possible for us. I agree with King David as he has written: **"You kings, be wise, be warned, you rulers of the earth: Serve the Lord with fear and rejoice with trembling…."** Psalm 2:12.

Chapter Six

We are looking at the Book of Revelation, chapter six. Here Jesus the Lamb of God, is opening the seals in a specific order. We will be surprised and may be puzzled that Jesus, as the meek Lamb is opening up actual judgments from God towards the inhabitants upon the earth.

The Lamb opened the second seal of the scroll. A fiery red horse with its rider came forth. The rider had a sword in his hand! He had the power to take peace from the earth and cause men slay each other. We know that because of greed and envy people want what other nations own. This horse and rider stir up violence and cause wars. It is not what God wants, but when humans do not deal with certain attitudes and sin, then this Rider will be released in that area.

Jesus, the Prince of Peace gives peace and the forgiveness of sin to those who receive him. But many Christians are persecuted for their faith. Jesus said 'Did I come to bring peace on earth?' Because of Him, brothers will betray each other. Families can come against one another because of their belief in Christ, for example Islam against Christianity, Catholics against Protestants and the Babylon-system of this world against the Bride of Christ.

Then the third seal was opened. A black horse came forth with a rider holding a pair of scales in his hands to weigh food: Indicating that food would become scarce. Usually after a war, food is difficult to come by. One action leads to another….

When the Lamb opened the fourth seal, John heard the fourth creature say 'Come!' and a pale horse rode forth. Its rider was named Death, and Hades was following close behind him. These spirits were given power to kill a fourth of the earth's population by sword, famine and wild beasts. This also reminds me of the time when the Israelites were to come out of Egypt. The angel of death went to the first born children of the Egyptians. Some critics will say 'But doesn't God love the Egyptians?' Yes, He does, but when leaders respond wrongly to God, that can cause a nation and their children to suffer. Men in leadership positions should not make decision according to their own desires, because their decisions will influence the outcome of their nation's welfare.

When the fifth seal was opened, John could see those who were killed because of their testimony about Jesus. We know that many Christians have suffered and died for their faith in Jesus. Take note that they were given white robes to wear and they have to wait for the full number of other believers to join them. We read in Daniel chapter seven verse twenty-five 'He will speak against the Most High and oppress the saints. The saints will be handed over to him for a time, times and half a time.' Here Daniel wrote about the anti-Christ who will persecute the saints, the chosen ones who serve/obey the Lord God. Who are they? Are they the Jews, Messianic Jews or Christians? I believe the saints are those from all nations who serve and trust in God.

As the sixth seal was opened, there was an earthquake. Stars fell from the sky! The sky receded like a scroll. Every mountain and island was removed from its place. Wow, what a shaking! The sun turned black and the moon was blood red. Although there have been many blood moons in the past years there was not an earthquake at the same time as a blood moon. So, this prophesy is not fulfilled yet. This will be the time when rulers and presidents will go into hiding. People will cry out to God. The great day of the wrath of God has come. Who can stand?

When the world is so full of sin, even nature suffers under the severity of unrighteousness. Therefore, the author of Romans

writes that even the earth longs for and cries out for the Sons of God to be revealed! The earth calls out for people to manage the world with love and justice. Saint Paul wrote that 'love is not happy when evil prevails'. Blessed is a nation when their King serves the Lord God. When there is peace and justice, even nature rejoices and blooms.

Chapter Seven

The Lord fulfills His plans for the Israelites. He led them out of Egypt. Later Jacob blessed his twelve sons. Such a blessing in faith lasts for generations. God watches over His word and the faith of a righteous man pleases God. God did not forget that prayer of blessing.

As we look at Revelation chapter seven, you will see that the descendants of Jacob, who was named Israel and the tribes of Israel, a remnant of the servants of God, will be kept safe by being sealed by the Holy Spirit. I believe they will be Messianic Jews and the Christians who obeyed and followed Jesus, their Rabbi and Savior.

Many critics complained that there are such a few servants. But when you read a bit further on you will read a joyful occurrence. **Multitudes of people, from every nation of the earth will stand before the Lamb dressed in white robes** (which are their good and righteous deeds), with palm branches in their hands, worshiping Jesus!

At first we see 144,000 servants of God, the first fruits and we get worried that we are not included. But this chapter shows us that God's eternal plan will be fulfilled. He chose the Jews first and then later He turned to the Gentile nations. **Those who were once not His people, are now called His own. Everybody who accepts Jesus, the perfect Lamb of God, will be saved.** So, all Israel will be saved. See Romans 11:25-27; Eph.2:11-19.

Then, one of the twenty four elders asked John 'Those in white robes- who are they and where did they come from?' John said: 'You know the answer'. The elder wanted John to take note of those people dressed in white so He answered **'These are they who have come out of the great tribulation. They have washed their robes...'** therefore they are day and night before the throne of God. They will never hunger nor thirst again. The Lamb will be their shepherd and lead them to springs of living water. He will wipe away every tear from their eyes. Hallelujah!

Between the opening of the six and the seven seal, we see a little bit of heaven. We see those who endured and stood strong in their faith. We see the multitude of worshipers. Man, I tell you, we need to be worshipers during that time! God is looking for true worshipers and here they are! You need to praise and worship God during the time of tribulation, during the time of testing. I suggest we start practicing now!

When the seven seal was opened, there was silence in heaven. Remember the shaking that took place when the six seal was opened. Now it was all quiet, but just for a while…. Seven angels blow their trumpets. Another angel poured out the incense of many prayers from a golden bowl before the throne of God. Please read chapter eight to get all the details. The purpose of my book is to share a message from the Book of Revelation to the readers. The message the Holy Spirit is revealing to me.

Sometimes believers might feel their prayers were not answered or it is not so important to God. In chapter eight, in the Book of Revelation, we read that our prayers are actually kept in a golden censer.

The seven angels blew their trumpets, each one after the other. Not together. As they blew, it had a major effect upon the earth. Great disasters! It is almost as in the days of Moses, when God punished the Egyptians, because of the stubbornness of their Pharaoh. But on a much larger scale, over the whole earth!

Hopefully, we as the saints will not be on the earth any longer. But we know we will also be tested. Jesus warned his disciples in Matthew 24:21 that there will come a very difficult time for everyone on the earth. I suggest, as we read the Book of Revelation, that we also look at the message Jesus shared with His disciples, written by Matthew.

With this, I concluded the first part of the message from the Book of Revelation. Soon, Lord willing, I shall write the second and third part, revealing the message of this wonderful book to a chosen generation!

Part Two

The Anti-Christ And Judgements

Chapter Eight

We are looking at the book of Revelation, written by the Apostle John, chapter eight and nine.

In these chapters we read many times about the number seven - seven seals, seven angels and seven trumpets! Interesting there are also seven Jewish feasts mentioned in the Old Scriptures which God commanded His people to keep. The feast of Tabernacle is the last feast in the year and starts with the sounding of trumpets. Tabernacle means to settle down, camp and relax amongst people. It symbolizes that Jesus come and lives/retires amongst His people. He makes his home on earth. During the millennium era, Jesus will reign with His winning saints, the 'Overcomers' for a thousand years on the earth, ruling the nations. Rev.20:4.

The angel with the golden censer captivated my attention. The angel poured out the prayers of all the saints upon the altar before the throne! Then the angel took the same censer filled with fire from the altar and hurled it to the earth. That caused thunder rumblings, flashes of lighting and also an earthquake!

The prayers of the righteous believers in Jesus, have a visible effect on the earth. The prayer of faith is really powerful. We know from the Book of Acts how the Christians prayed for Peter while he was imprisoned. God sent an angel to set him free. Also whilst Paul and Silas worshipped in prison, there was an earthquake and their chains broke off.

While I was on a mission in Campbletown, Scotland, God ordered me to go and read a passage of scripture – standing on a hill – overlooking the village. While I was reading, there were flashes of lighting and rumbling of thunders, confirming God's powerful word from the book of Isaiah.

The Spirit-filled prayers of the saints can change the face of the earth. I am reminded that it is written in Isaiah 32:15 that when the Spirit of God moves over a desert, it becomes a fertile land.

One of my mentors, Gerda Leitgob, a prayer warrior, was directed by the Holy Spirit to contact a church leader in one of the villages in Quatamala. He told her that for some reason his church was suffering the loss of many members. So Gerda felt led to go and investigate the problem and teach the few members how to pray.

When she arrived in the poor village, she saw the almost naked children roaming the dirty streets. They looked sick and underfed. She taught the people how to pray with authority … how to 'govern' their village. At the end of her training, they also approached the witch who lived up on the hill, overlooked their village. After they have confronted her with God's word, she fled the village. Overnight, the atmosphere in the village changed. She had hurled down curses on the Church, which was one of the reasons why it became empty. While Gerda was there, the members came back and the church started to fill up again. In a short time, more than 300 members started to regularly attend the Church.

After a few years, Gerda went back to the same village and was pleasantly surprised to see the children well dressed and playing in clean streets. The poor farmers she met the previous time were driving Mercedes trucks full of their own vegetations for export. They were prospering spiritually, but also physically!

Gerda took pictures of their products: tomatoes as big as the inside of a man's hands! The carrots were as large as the length of an adult's arm - from the hand to the elbow. I saw it with my own eyes! The children were not sick and sad anymore, but joyful. Prayers filled with the Holy Spirit, changes the face of a land - a nation!

The land of Israel also has a story of her own, about how a desert became a fruitful garden - but spiritually they need feeding. Their laws cannot save them; Moses cannot save them and their 'Tora' cannot give them eternal life. But the Lord of Moses, and the Author of the Scriptures can save them - Jesus Christ is his Name, the Savior of this world! That is what Isaiah prophesied in his book Chapter 32: 15&16.

In chapters eight and nine of the Book of Revelations, we read about the seven silver trumpets sounding, calling the nations to repent and turn from their wicked ways, turn back to God to have a living relationship with him - Elohim, the creator of the universe. In the prophetic book **of Amos, chapter three**, we read when a trumpet sounds in a city, who does not tremble and when a disaster comes to a city, has not the Lord caused it? We read in verse seven, that **the Sovereign Lord does nothing without revealing his plan to his servants the prophets.** The Lord God told Jonah to warn the city of Nineveh that He was about to destroy, unless they repented! The Governor of the city listened, yielded and called everyone to humble themselves. God relented and spared the people from disaster.

Angels sounded the trumpets: Which I believe are not real sounds, but natural disasters that will have an impact on the world, making the news headlines.

At the **first trumpet** sound, hail and fire mixed with blood was hurled down upon the earth. A third of the earth, trees and grass were burned up!

At the **second trumpet** sound, something like a huge mountain (a possible asteroid) ablaze hit the sea! A third of the sea creatures died and a third of the ships were destroyed.

At the **third trumpet** sound: A huge blazing star (called Wormwood) fell from the sky on a third of the rivers. Springs of water turn bitter and many people died.

Actually it is very difficult for me to write these near future disasters, as I would like to believe I am a messenger of Good News. So please read for yourself what is written in the book of Revelation, especially from chapters 8 to 18 as I will just give the message the Holy Spirit revealed to me for today's generation.

In the news today, people are complaining about drastic weather changes/patterns and are really moody about it. Wait until they read about this - as a loving father disciplines his son to come in line with his will, so God is calling the nations to pay attention, to make right with Him - but will they yield, will they repent?

The **fourth Angel** sounded the trumpet: A third of the sun, the moon and stars were struck, so that a third of day and night will have no light. Such darkness will cover the earth!

Like the increase of birth pangs, so shall natural disasters increase. The last three trumpets are last warnings, calling people to repentance. Just like in the times of Moses in Egypt, when he wanted Pharaoh to let God's people go. The sounding of the trumpets, are like a call for the release people from the clutches of this world to enter the spiritual ark of God, His Spiritual Kingdom.

An eagle flying in mid- air calls out 'Woe, woe, woe' to the inhabitants on the earth, as the three last warning trumpets are about to sound….

The fifth angel sounded the trumpet - a star falls on the earth and cause a very deep cut into the earth, opening up the Abyss. This will cause locust to rise from the hole and inflict harm on those people who are not sealed by the Holy Spirit.

The sixth angel sounded the trumpet and a voice from the horns of the golden altar commanded the released of the four angels from Euphrates River, to kill a third of mankind.

We read in Revelation 9:20 – That the rest of mankind that were not killed by these plagues still did not repent of the works of their hands: the idols of gold, silver, bronze, stone and wood – idols that cannot see or hear or walk. Neither did they repent of murders, magic acts, their sexual immorality or thefts.

It is now the time to repent! Blessed are those who wash their clothes and yield to the voice of the Holy Spirit as it is written in Chapters Two and Three. While it is still 'Day' we have the opportunity to go and buy the extra oil, being sealed and filled with the Holy Spirit.

Do not wait till darkness covers the earth, then it will be too late to fill your lamps with oil before the night comes. (Read Matt.25)

Chapter Ten

In this chapter we shall look at Chapters twelve and thirteen of the book Revelation from a Biblical viewpoint.

I believe in Chapter 12 of the book of Revelation, the "woman" John saw, was not a person but she represents the hidden Bride of Christ on mother earth. He saw a wondrous sign in heaven.

We read in Genesis one, the book that Moses wrote through the revelation he received from God how He created the universe. In verse fourteen he wrote that God made the stars to serve as signs to mark seasons and years. I remembered in the book doctor Luke wrote, he mentioned how the wise men saw a bright star and they knew something important was about to happen: A King was to be born.

The first time, in verse five of the book of Revelations, the woman represents the time of the Virgin birth of Jesus. Joseph took Mary and Baby Jesus and fled to Egypt as King Herod wanted to kill Him. Then secondly, it could be what Apostle Paul saw in the Spirit, the time of the birth of the One New man, he mentioned in his letter to the Galatians, chapters 3:24-4:7.

The Jews and Gentiles become one holy nation, the chosen believers in Jesus Christ! Romans 11:13-24.

And thirdly, the dragon, the devil will also go after and try to kill the chosen generation at the end of the church age, before the return of the Righteous Ruler, King Jesus!

I believe in chapter 12 we read about the warfare against the devil in the spiritual realm with the Arch-angel Michael. Since the devil was hurled down to earth, Christians are able to overcome him by the "Blood of the Lamb and the word of our testimony". Those who are one with Christ, who have received His Gift of Life, through His sacrificial blood, can withstand the attacks of the devil. When we wear the full amour, of which Paul wrote to the church in Ephesus, and have the Word of God in our mouths, we can have victory over the lies and threats of the devil!

In chapter thirteen, we read about the beast that will come out of the sea. The sea usually represents the nations which are link together; at the time when this prophetic book was written, trading and missionary ships connected continents with one another. I believe the beast coming from the sea is a reproduction from old serpent, satan, the Father of lies and deception, the Prince of the Air that connect countries and leaders today, like the internet. This beast has many heads, who are the leaders under satan's influence. One head will become the Anti-christ. We already know that the dragon is satan and he gives power to the beast. The beast is like a leopard that blends in with his environments; he gains ground like a bear- slowly but surely and speaks with authority, like a lion, intimidating and threatening. One of the heads of the beast (a leader) had a fatal wound (it could've been a tumor or perhaps a bullet wound) but then somebody else must have ministered healing to him. The world will be in awe about this "miracle", but this beast speaks arrogantly and blasphemes God! Take note: He will slander the Lord's Name, His dwelling place (the places of worship) and the angels in heaven. He will make war against God's holy people; the saints and overpower them! I suggest you also read Daniel chapter 7:25 onwards. Personally, I believe that the beast will be encouraged by the media and television. They will blaspheme the Lord's Name, which is Jesus. The world media will come up against God's people. This is sad to read that the church/Christians did not exercise their rightful authority over the beast. On the other hand, Jesus also suffered and died before He was resurrected. But then we read in the book of Daniel 7:27 the good news that eventually all the kingdoms of the world will be ruled by the Kingdom of God!

I see there is another beast coming from the earth. This beast causes that the inhabitants worship the first beast. Please understand the word "Worship" —meaning focus on; give your valuable time to and think about it most of the time; be devoted to; obey its demands on your life. The second beast, I believe will come from a manmade system. It could be a government with the help of technology to manipulate all nations to receive the mark of the beast. The mark has three sixes. According to Hebrew numerical, six is the number of man: the sinful, fleshly, natural animal nature. We read in Romans chapter 8 that we must crucify the physical nature and replace it with a godly, spiritual character. Therefore, we must be baptized with the Hoy Spirit to be spiritually connected with Christ. God is spirit and our fleshly nature cannot fellowship with the Holy Spirit.

When I was in my final year, studying Biblical studies, in 1979, I asked the Lord: What is the mark of the beast? The Book of Revelations was then my assignment for my final marks. The Bible says: If anyone lacks wisdom, one can ask for wisdom and He will grant it. So, I asked for wisdom. I few days later, I was asked to cook a meal for our fellowship group. I went down to the local shop to buy a chicken. As I reached for it, the Holy Spirit pointed out to me the barcode and said that when the bar-code gets in or unto the human skin, that will be the mark of the beast! I believe the number 666 could be your birth-date, an area number and your bank sort code. Yes, it is the number of mankind, your personal number to buy and sell without cash! So, I asked the Lord why we must not take the code and have a chip on hands or forehead? I heard God the Holy Spirit say that; **"We are bought with a price, by the Blood of Jesus Christ! Our bodies are the Temple of the Holy Spirit and we do not belong to a world system of buying and selling! We are holy and belong to the King of Kings and His spiritual Kingdom."**

Why people and a world generation would accept the Anti-Christ, is because satan and his helpers create chaos on purpose, so that nations will long for a leader who can create order. He will come as one who desire to do good, fits in with the longings and the needs of society. He will be able to do magic acts/tricks, inspired by the occult which so many people find fascinating on television these days. He could be trans-gender as the Bible says he has no natural desire towards women, or respect the marriage covenant as God instituted. He will be against Christians, especially evangelist as they will be too narrow-minded. According to the one world religion and government, we must just accept everybody with sin and madness. This is the false prophet. Do not disturb the so called "peace" in the community, until he calls the shots! Until he has influences everyone to accept and worship the first beast, the Anti-Christ. The false prophet, who will twist the truth, just like satan did with Adam and Eve then, he will do it again world-wide through the media, deceiving the nations. What is evil, he will call "freedom or progress" and when it comes to people: we must accepts people's choice and weaknesses, show more grace/love and tolerance for sin and that which is good, he will call it "old fashion or fundamental" and when it comes to people with faith: " those narrow-minded evangelicals!"

But for those who are wise (Matt.25) and are filled and sealed with the Holy Spirit, will not bow their knee to a false god. They will not receive the mark of the beast. They will put their hope and trust in the living God; not the god that human's fashion by hand; But the God who made the heavens and the earth, is also my God who can save humans from damnation and eternal hell.

Chapter Eleven

We will now look at the Book of Revelation's chapters fourteen, fifteen and sixteen, which consist of the judgments on the rebellious people.

In the previous chapter, we read that some people will receive the mark of the beast, but here in front of the Lamb stood 144,000 saints with the Name of the Lamb and the Fathers name on their forehead. Jacob, the son of Isaac, had twelve sons, who became the twelve tribes of Israel. According to the Hebrew numerals, twelve is the number of government. Thus, I believe the 144,000 are the first fruit so to speak; the remnant of Christians from every tribe. They were redeemed from the earth. Which could mean that God took them "home" before the rest of all the other believers. John also wrote that they were men (and women) that did not live sexually immoral but lived pure and blameless lives like a Daniel. They did not lie but lived righteous and holy as God requires.

It seems when John wrote, he wrote to men because females weren't taught to read in those days and when he wrote about men, he meant mankind (male and female).

They sang a new song when they stood before the throne and the four living creatures (mentioned in chapter four) and the 24 elders. This vision was in heaven where God's throne is.

Then John saw an angel who, flying in midair, proclaimed the eternal gospel to every nation, tribe and language of people. He said: "**Fear God and give him glory of the hour of judgment has come. Worship him who made the heavens, the earth, sea and springs of water!**"

There is a second angel who announced the fall of Babylon. And then a third angel proclaimed in a loud voice: "**If anyone worships the beast and his image and receives the mark of the beast on the forehead or hand, he too will drink the wine of God's fury from the cup of his wrath. He will be tormented with burning sulfur in the presence of the holy angels and of the Lamb. And the smoke of their torment rises forever and ever. There is no rest day or night for those who worship the beast and his image or for anyone who receives the mark of his name.**"

Please take careful note of` verse twelve: During that time of the Anti-christ and people receiving the mark of the beast, the saints must stay patient, obey God's commands and remain faithful to Jesus. Then John heard a voice from heaven: "Blessed are the dead who die in the Lord from now on." Meaning: It is better to die than to live during the time of tribulation. And the Spirit agrees, saying "Yes, they will rest from their labour, for their deeds will follow them."

John saw a white cloud and seated on the cloud was one 'like a son of man' with a crown on his head. An angel who came out of the temple in heaven called to the one on the cloud to take the sickle and swing it over the earth, for the harvest of the earth is ripe. The angels are the harvesters. We need to read Matthew 13:37-43 to compare with this chapter. At the time of the harvest, the angels will first gather out of God's Kingdom those people who hinder and apposed His Lordship. Remember the Kingdom of God is coming down to earth! Therefore, at that time of the harvest, at end of the Church age, the angels will be very active in establishing God's Kingdom on earth. They will separate the good wheat from the tares; the sheep from the goats and the good fish from the bad ones according to the parables of God's kingdom.

John saw seven angels with seven plagues to complete God's wrath towards the ungodly on the earth. The angels were dressed in clean, shining linen and wore golden sashes across their chests. He also saw those who were victorious over the beast and his mark and image, standing beside a sea of glass mixed with fire. God gave them harps to play and they sang the song of Moses and the Lamb:

> **Great and marvelous are your deeds,**
> **Lord Almighty.**
> **Just and true are your ways,**
> **King of the ages.**
> **Who will not fear you, O the Lord,**
> **and bring glory to your Name?**
> **For You alone are holy.**
>
> **All nations will come and**
> **worship before you,**
> **for your acts of righteousness have been revealed.**

John also saw the temple in heaven, called the tabernacle of Testimony was opened. (Rev.15:5). Out of the temple came the angels with the last seven plagues:

1.The first angel pours out his bowl on the land. Painful and ugly soars broke out on the people who took the mark of the beast and worship his image.

2. The second angel pours out his bowl on the sea. The sea water turn into dark color of old blood and every living thing died in the sea.

3. The third angel poured out his bowl on the rivers and springs of water and they become blood. The angel said that God is just in His judgments as they had shed the blood of God's servants, the prophets and His saints. And it was confirmed by those at the altar.

4. The fourth angel poured out his bowl of the wrath of God on the sun. The sun scorched the people and the heat was intense so that they cursed the name of God who control the plagues. But they refused to repent and honour Him. You see, children who were not trained to submit to authority or honor their parents, will struggle to obey an unseen God. Adults who are self righteous and full of pride/arrogance, they will not acknowledge God and will therefore suffer.

5. The firth angel poured his bowl over the throne of the beast. His place of authority was plunged into darkness. They were in pain and agony, but still did not seek the Lord, nor repent of their wrong doings.

6. The sixth angel pour out his bowl on the Euphrates river (runs from east Turkey, over Iraq and mouth out near Kuweit city) so that the water dried up to prepare the way for the armies of the East to come across to the land Israel. At that time, evil spirits

will come out of the mouth of the dragon, the beast and the false prophet to gather all the political leaders from the whole world to fight God's holy people. They will gather at a place called Armageddon.

7. The seventh angel poured out his bowl into the air and a loud voice cried out from the temple: It is done! There will be a severe earthquake, the largest and most tremendous that the great city split in three parts (Jerusalem?) and the city of the nations (Dubai or London perhaps) will collapse! Babylon will fall and every island will go down and even mountains will be leveled. So the whole world will be shaken and islands will disappear. From the sky, huge hail stones, about a hundred pounds each will fall on people. People will curse God because the plague was so terrible!

Chapter Twelve

We are looking in Revelation, chapter seventeen at the harlot who is riding the first beast, who came out of the sea. We know that the sea stands for the nations, people and languages. But who is the woman? The previous chapter, the woman who fled with her child to Egypt, was the church, the pure Bride of Christ. At the end of chapter seventeen of the book of Revelation, it says that the harlot is a city. A city, with a group of people that have and will have great influence over nations and people and languages. A city with a man-made institute or a governmental order which is run by influential leaders.

The whore is Named: **Mystery – Babylon the Great- The Mother of Prostitutes and of the Abomination of the earth!** The word "Mystery" says to me it is a spiritual matter that must be revealed to us. Babylon the Great – Babylon always relates to human empowerment, the exhortation of man's abilities, idols, instead of honoring the Almighty God. The Mother of prostitutes – which is the driving force behind prostitution – self-indulgence of the flesh and the lack of the Holy Spirit in one's life.

The abomination in this world is when man changes the natural laws God made, rebels against God's order and takes a position in as God.

All the above is one and the same spirit as Jezebel!

We read about her in the time of King Ahab and the Prophet Elijah. We read again in the book of Revelation how this "women" which could be a male figure too, influences the church towards sexual immorality. To me this is the same "women" spurring the nations on to sin against God and his natural laws and order.

This harlot drives people to fornicate with the gods of this world, who misled kings to make wrong decisions in killing the innocent, like Herodias asked for the head of John the Baptist. That voice of deception that killed so many Jews, Christians and children. That 'voice' that told mothers they have a right to kill their innocent babies while in the womb. The perverse spirit that confuses children and youth of their gender identity! It is this Jezebel spirit who influenced the false prophets to tell the world we should accept gays and lesbians as a lifestyle choice and allow them to get married in church! It is this same spirit who killed the prophets in the time of Elijah and those religious leaders who killed Jesus, out of jealousy and fear. It is that spirit that killed the Christians in Rome by feeding them to the lions for fun and that spirit who spurred on the Catholic Church to persecute the Protestants that were seeking to live a Holy life. Thousands died under the hand of the so called "Church"- which I believe is not the true church or Body of Christ, but the counterfeit, the man-made religious institution. Verse six said it: "I saw that the woman was drunk with the blood of the saints, the blood of those who bore testimony of Jesus! We know today that satan, the dragon himself was behind all those murders and persecution. The father of lies and deception, who come to kill, steal and destroy.

Dr. Henry Halley made an in-depth study on the history and origin of the Catholic Church. He is convinced that the "harlot" is this mother church. Instead of doing the good deeds Jesus did on earth, they enriched themselves, enlarge their territory for their own power and lived immoral lives. (See Halley's Bible Handbook pages 778-781) For example Pius II had many illegitimate children and taught young men how to seduce women. Paul II filled his home with concubines and Innocent VIII had 16 children from various married women! Just to mention a few Popes immoral lives. We also know from history how many people were killed and burned at the stake for their sincere beliefs, such as translating the Bible into people's own language like John Huss.

Now the good news: We read that the nations will hate the harlot. Why? Because the harlot manipulated, humiliated, drove and control people into doing things against their inner conviction. One of the seven angels showed John the punishment the woman who sat on the first beast would receive. The nations will turn against her, ruin her and completely burn her. Just as King Jehu made an end of Queen Jezebel according to 2 Kings 9:20- 37. "**How can there be peace', Jehu replied, "as long as all the idolatry and witchcraft of your mother Jezebel abounds?**" The name of this harlot is Babylon, a city that controlled the kings of the earth.

In Chapter eighteen of the Book of Revelation, we read about the ruin of Babylon, the great city that controlled the kings of the earth. This city became a home of demons and a haunt of evil spirits. You see when people moved away from God and believe they are superior to God, they open themselves up to the work of the devil. Babylon relied on her own strength and abilities. She had no relationship with the living God. Oh, she acknowledged that there is a God, so did the devil and his demons too, but Babylon did not obey or worship the Living God who made the heavens and the earth.

John heard another voice from heaven cried: "**Come out of her, my people, so that you will not share in her sins, so that you will not receive any of her plagues**" This city will be burnt to the ground. The city must be a coastal city that is now trading and shipping large cargoes to other countries. John wrote: "O great city, dressed in fine linen, purple and scarlet and glittering gold" That is why many authors believe it is the Vatican City of Rome as those cardinals dressed in red and wearing gold. I believe it is describing a real city, but at the same time represents the common wealth of the world, made by wrong means and methods and not according to the Way; the laws of the Kingdom of God. As God's kingdom comes, man-made kingdoms will fall!

Another mighty angel demonstrated prophetically how the city will be frown down as he picked up a boulder and threw it into the sea! Within a very short time, within one hour, I believe literally, the city will be destroyed!

In that city prophets and saints were killed. This again reminds us of how many Christians were martyred in varies continents. From out of that city the decision will be made to kill all those who will not receive the mark of the beast, during the time of the tribulation. More reason for people to read this little book and then read the biblical book of Revelation which I have clarified while writing this important message.

My question to church leaders, pastors and shepherds is: Are your sheep in a safe place? Are your watchmen awake and standing ready to sound alarm, as the watchman of old blew the rams-horn; the shofar? Listen, the angels are sounding the trumpets! Gather the sheep, bring them into the fold. The night has come!

I believe that while people are still reading this little booklet, the "scroll," it will be the time of the tribulation. They will see these things happening, but for those whose names are written in the Book of Life, for you who call on the Name of the Lord: Jesus Christ, you shall be saved!

Part Three

The Return of Jesus Christ!

Chapter Thirteen

In this chapter we are looking at the Coming King. This will be an over view of chapters nineteen to twenty two of the Book of Revelation.

We read in the previous chapter that God will judge Babylon, the harlot city. John wrote: "**Rejoice over her, O heaven! Rejoice, saints and apostles and prophets! God has judged her for the way she treated you**". In one hour she has been brought to ruin! There was a roar of a great multitude shouting: Hallelujah! Salvation and glory and power belong to our God and true and just are His judgments. He has condemned the great prostitute who corrupted the earth by her adulteries. God has avenged on her for the blood of His saints!

Apostle John heard another roar of rushing waters and pearls of thunder, shouting: "**Hallelujah, for our Lord God Almighty reigns. Let us rejoice and be glad and give Him glory, for the wedding of the Lamb has come, and his bride has made herself ready! Fine linen, bright and clean linen was given her to wear**".

The servants of God were given clothes, because during the tribulations of their time of testing, (They kept their faith, stayed loyal to Jesus, endured hardship) their clothes got dirty and they could not buy new clothes. They might have been beaten and blood stains had soiled their old clothes. They might be in pain, hurting and hungry ... They were given white linen, because they behaved and did right in God's eyes. This passage also reminds me of the parable Jesus told that the kingdom of God is like a wedding feast. (Matt.22) Remember the church in Sardis. Jesus promised them and said that those who overcome, will walk with Him, dressed in white. You will be given the right outfit for the wedding of the Lamb!

John saw in heaven a rider on a white horse. The rider is called: Faithful and True. We know that the Spirit of Truth is the Holy Spirit and faithfulness is a fruit of the Holy Spirit.(Galatians 5:22) He is riding on behalf of Truth and is faithful to His conquest! Jesus confessed: "**My food is to do the will of my Father**", and King David wrote about this coming King of kings in Psalm 45:4. "**In your majesty, ride forth victoriously on behalf of truth, humility and righteousness...**" The rider's name is the Word of God! John wrote in chapter 1 of his Gospel: "In the beginning was the Word and the Word was with God and the Word was

God." And the Word became flesh and made his dwelling among us. John is referring to Jesus, the first born Son of God.

"His eyes are like blazing fire." It is the same eyes John saw in chapter 1. And on his thigh He has his other Names written: **"King of kings and Lord of lords!"** With Him, the armies of heaven were following, riding on white horses and dressed in fine white linen. Who are they, these armies of heaven? We just read that the servants of God were given white linen clothes. We read in the previous chapter that God delivered His first fruits, the 144,000, before the angels poured out the wrath of God on the earth. Thus during the tribulations these "first fruits" went to be with God in heaven and came back with Jesus as part of the armies of heaven to rule the nations with the iron sceptre as Jesus said in Rev. 2:27.

This is the time when the beast and other kings want to make war against Jesus and His army. But the beast was captured, and also the false prophet was thrown in the lake of fire. The rest were struck with the sword coming from the mouth of the Rider on the white horse. Meaning they were judged by the Word of God. Daniel also wrote down this prophecy in Daniel chapter 7:26, 27. **"Then the sovereignty, power and greatness of the kingdoms will be hand over to the saints, the people of**

the Most High. His kingdom will be an everlasting kingdom and all rulers will worship and obey Him."

John saw an angel coming down from heaven with a key and a great chain in his hands. He seized the dragon, the ancient serpent, who is the devil or satan and bound him for a thousand years. He threw him in the Abyss, sealed it so he could not deceive the nations for a thousand years.

He saw the thrones of those who had been given authority to judge and he saw the souls of those who were beheaded for sharing about Jesus and did not receive the mark on their foreheads or hands. They came to life and reign with Christ for a thousand years.

After a thousand years, satan is released. He will go around the world to deceive again and gather a large army to fight against God's people and the city He loves. That must be Jerusalem which I love too! But fire will came down from heaven and devour them. This time the devil was thrown in the lake of fire where the false prophet and the beast were thrown in as well.

Then John saw a white throne and Him who was seated on it. Earth and sky rolled up – fled from His presence (disappeared) He must have been so huge and awesome! The dead came alive, great and small and were judge according to what they have done as recorded in the books! Death and Hades were also thrown in the lake of fire, which is the second death. Please take careful note: **If anyone's name was not found written in the book of Life, they were thrown in the lake of fire!**

In chapter twenty one, John wrote in his book of Revelation that the first heaven and earth had passed away and there was no longer a sea! We read that God created a new earth; and that the earth has changed so much that a different earth was created, which I believe will be spiritual, because God is Spirit and when He dwells amongst us, it must be a spiritual place where He is at home.

John saw the Holy City, the New Jerusalem coming down out of heaven (not man made, but created by God) prepared AS a bride (just as a bride would be dressed beautifully for her wedding day) But the Holy City is not the "Bride of Christ," it is the place God made for his true Bride we read about in chapter nineteen, verse seven. The saints who are wearing clean white linen, those Believers who has prepared themselves for the coming King, are the Bride of Christ.

God will dwell and live with His people in this New Jerusalem. He will wipe away all their sadness and there will be no more madness, but only gladness because there will be no more pain or death in the new earth. He who was seated on the throne said: "**I am making everything new!**" He said to John: "**It is done. I am the Alpha and Omega, the Beginning and the End. To him who is thirsty, I will give to drink without cost from the spring of the water of Life. He who overcomes will inherit all this and I will be his God and he will be my son ...**" Reading these words, we know it is King Jesus who was speaking, because Jesus said those same words recorded in John's gospel when Jesus cried out at the feast in old Jerusalem: "**If anybody is thirsty, come and drink without cost!**" We also know Jesus said that he and the Father is One; when you see Jesus you also see God the Father. (John 14:9).

In the beginning of this book we read about Jesus warning the churches to repent of their sins of the flesh and idolatry that was waging war against the kingdom of God. Jesus encourages us that when we overcome the world and our fleshly weaknesses, we shall inherit all these promises. You see, there is a reward for those who obey the voice of God and also obey the written word of God! It is written: "**But the cowardly, the**

unbelieving, the vile, the murderers, the sexually immoral, those who practice magic arts, the idolaters and liars- their place will be in the fiery lake of burning sulphur. This is the second death."

The New Jerusalem is made of precious stones and you can read the description in Rev.21:10-21. The twelve gates of the Holy city were made of pearls and the street was made of pure gold, like transparent glass. I can easily believe it, because I saw the sea of glass in the heavenly place which was described in the Holy Scriptures.

John did not see a temple in this city, because the Lord God Almighty and the Lamb is its temple. The city does not need the sun or moon to provide light, because the glory of God provides the light! The nations will walk by its light/glory and the kings of the (new) earth will bring their splendour (glory and honour) into it. Nothing impure will ever enter it nor anyone what does what is shameful of deceitful, but only those whose names are written in the Lamb's book of life.

Let us carefully consider, meditate on the above paragraph. What kind of people ought we to be to be able to walk in the New Jerusalem?! Yes, unfortunately in the past we were taught that we must only believe and be at ease, God does the rest... that is why so many Christians do nothing for God's kingdom. But when you have a relationship with the living God, you can and will also produce life! Jesus expects to see good fruit in our lives! Paul wrote that God predestined us to do the works He has pre-planned for us – it is for us to walk in obedience according to God's purpose for our lives! To be in a relationship with God is a key-factor. Did anyone, your parents or a spiritual leader/mentor teach you how to obey God? Do people expect to just fly into heaven and go and sit at the wedding table to be served?! Jesus paid with his holy life for you to be in that special relationship with Almighty God. What are you doing with that Gift of Life - the free voucher to have the abundant life, eternally? You could exchange your old carnal mind and body for the new life with Christ. He shall make you a new being; a person who can connect spiritually with God. (2 Cort.5:17.)

An angel showed John a crystal clear river of life flowing from the throne of God and the Lamb, down in the middle of the street. The tree of Life stem and roots grows over on both sides of the river, bearing twelve crops of fruit in a year; bearing fruit each month! And the leaves are for the healing of the nations. I believe this is the same tree of Life that grew in the time of

Adam and Eve in the Garden of Eden. God's servants will have His name on their foreheads and they will see Him!

The angel said: "These words are trustworthy and true. (Revering to the book of Revelation) The Lord, the God of the spirits of the prophets sent his angel to show his servants the things that must soon take place. Do not seal up the words of the prophecy of this book, because the time is near. Let him who does wrong, continue to do wrong, let him who is vile, continue being vile; let him who does right continue to do right; and let him who is holy continue to be holy." This doesn't meant, people should not repent and change; no – he meant during the time of "Jacobs troubles", evangelism and preaching will cease, then the saints must stay steadfast and watch their own lives to endure until they see the Lord's Face to face. And those who chose to rebel and ignored the Gospel, willfully sinned and chose not turn to God – they will be killed with the sword that come out of the mouth of the rider on the horse. (Rev.19:21)

"Behold, I am coming soon! My reward is with me and I will give to everyone according to what he has done. Blessed are those who wash their robes that they may eat from the tree of Life and may enter into the city." But outside the city are the dogs, those who practice magic arts, the sexual immoral, the murderers, the idolaters, and everyone who loves to lie and deceives.

"**I, Jesus have sent my angel to give you this testimony for the churches. I am the root and the Offspring of David and the bright Morning star**". The Spirit and the bride say "Come!" And let him who hears say, "Come" Whoever is thirsty, let him come and whoever wishes, let him take the free gift of the water of life! Amen.

Acknowledgement

I would like to thank Valerie Taylor for her encouragement to write this book and for help editing the first part of the book. Many thanks to Rev. Dennis Lloyd for shown interest in my work and helped me with the grammar editing.
A heartfelt thank you to my daughter-in-law for her beautiful design of the Cover pages!
A special thanks to my companion and faithful friend Roy, for choosing the right words and compiling this much needed book for this generation.
I am grateful and value everyone's time that helped me to complete this book. Finally, I would like to acknowledge other authors and their Books who inspired me and gave me clarification on my own revelations that I received from the Holy Spirit: Such as —

Hal Lindsay – "There's a New World Coming"

Dr. Henry Halley's Bible Handbook.

David C. Pack – "Revelation Explained at last!"

Rev. Clarence Larkin - "Dispensational Truth".

Dr. Arnold G. Fruchtenbaum – "The Footsteps of the Messiah"

Life Application Bible – New International Version.

The Holy Bible – Gideon's International in the British Isles

All praise, honor and glory to Jesus, our coming King!

Printed in Poland
by Amazon Fulfillment
Poland Sp. z o.o., Wrocław

56373915R00047